Excuse Your Excuses

Excuse Your Excuses

Lakhila Tellis

Copyright © 2021 by Lakhila Tellis.

All rights reserved.

No part of this book may be reproduced or transmitted in any form or by any means, electronic or mechanical, including photocopying, recording, or by any information storage and retrieval system, without permission in writing from the copyright author, except for the use of brief quotations in a book review.

ISBN: 978-1-970135-80-0 Paperback
      978-1-970135-81-7 Hardcover
      978-1-970135-82-4 Ebook

Published in the United States by Pen2Pad Ink Publishing.

Requests to publish work from this book or to contact the author should be sent to: iconicvoices@gmail.com

Lakhila Tellis retains the rights to all images.

Dedication

I dedicate this book to my loving and courageous mother, Lydia Denese Tellis-Jackson, and my amazing grandmother Evangelist Queen Esther Miller. You two are the strongest women who have taught me to love, to forgive and to have faith. May you continue to be the angels that watch over me, the arms to hold me when I feel alone, and the wings to carry me when I feel weak.

To my children, Keshawn, Keith, LaKhiya and LaKai: Mommy loves you all so much! You all give me strength and so much joy. I am blessed to have such beautiful, unique and loving children. We are a team. Always remember: Believe in yourself, and you can make the impossible possible!

To my brothers: Keith and Kardell. Thank you for being by my side. I cherish the time we spend and all the laughs. I love you guys so much. I definitely thank you for always letting your big sister feel like a queen!

Table of Contents

Introduction	11
Preface	13
Chapter 1: Yesterday	15
Chapter 2: Choices	34
Chapter 3: Love Yourself	50
Chapter 4: Unique	65
Chapter 5: Be Great	73
Bonus: Tips for you	82
Get Connected	84

Introduction

Hello readers! I welcome you to join me as I jump out my comfort zone. I have a great desire to help those like myself shine brighter than rays of sunshine on a hot summer day in July. I understand that everyone who reads this may not have the same issues, but I welcome you just the same. The principles presented in this book can be applied to your daily relation ships - personal and business. Either way, I hope and pray I can help you do so. Too often we lack hearing words of encouragement and support of loved ones along with faith in God, our dreams, and self. I choose to share my story to uplift you and encourage you. You define what success and happiness looks like for you. I hope this book helps you to create and maintain the vision you have for your life.

Excuse Your Excuses

Preface

There is no day better than today to start my story. I dedicated a lot of time to personal development. I am always learning. As I learn, I become stronger and more confident. As an adult, I know that I am special, important, and destined for greatness. I envision myself receiving recognition for my accomplishments. Question is...what will I do? I am merely a nurse. I do what I am supposed to do as a nurse. That requires no special salute. As I continue this journey, I realize there is so much more to me and the power of the mind.

I choose to tell my story to inspire at least one other person. A broken heart is difficult to mend. Yet, it is so powerful once it has healed. I know what it feels like to feel weak, alone, and misunderstood. I also know what it feels like to be strong, to persevere through adversity, and to love myself.

Now my question for you is where are you in life? Mentally. Physically.

Financially. Where do you want to be? Stop making excuses and go get "it"! Every excuse you use to disqualify yourself is every reason you need to go for your dreams, heal your heart, and serve *your* purpose!

Chapter 1

Yesterday

Yesterday: on the day last part; on the day preceding today

I remember the day I had to make real choices like it was yesterday. My life changed, and I had absolutely no control. Or so I thought. It was awkward. It was eerie. That moment was so strange. I entered a dimly lit room filled with family sitting in a circle and all sad faces but no spoken words. I was confused and concerned. "Where is my mother?" I asked. There was a short period of silence. That single moment of silence actually seemed like hours. I honestly cannot remember the exact words my grandmother said. I remember asking questions: Why didn't anyone tell me? Why did you guys let me go on with my day?

How could they let me come home

and find out my mother died while I was at school? My heart broke for the first time that day. I was 15 years old: 4 months away from my bittersweet sixteen.

That night I knew things would be different. I could not wrap my head around what happened. My mother had died unexpectedly due to natural causes. I went to the doctor with my mother the day before. I could not understand why she died. She was fine *yesterday*.

I cannot fathom anyone waking up to a normal day and returning home to a tragic nightmare. Yet, I experienced it. I was shattered. I never experienced loss so close to me. I did not understand it. I officially understood death. I could not understand what just happened to my life. I spent my final days with my mother.

Why me? Why us? Why my mother? I needed her. I was too young. My brothers were too young. No one could love us or care for us like Mama. I was at a very vulnerable age. So many thoughts ran through my mind constantly. It was overwhelming.

As I began life without my mother, I

had to decide how I would live my life. Would I finish school? Would I start dating? Would I go to college? I decided to take advantage of my situation. I was lost, empty, and rebellious. I decided to be wild and free. I was like some of the other girls in my neighborhood. I was raised and taught to be better than what I displayed. I wanted to have fun, run the streets, smoke weed, drink, and stay out late. I did just that.

Honestly, I was definitely not free. I was trapped in my feelings. I was so impulsive. I perceived it as being carefree. In reality, I was careless.

I would travel alone from Chicago by train to see my best friend in Kenosha, WI. No one knew where I was going most of the time. I spent late nights in the streets with whoever would keep me company. A lot of times I hung out with my female friends and hunted for boys. I would go places and do things that truly jeopardized my safety.

I was disrespectful to my mind, my body, and my soul. I made myself believe these were the things that I wanted to do.

Things I needed to enjoy my life. In doing so, I led myself to danger. I did not know it then, but the state I was in had me out of sync with reality.

One of the things that really changed me was so difficult to accept. I was raped three separate times by three different men. These are memories that I have tried to bury for years. Two out of three of those times I was with someone I trusted. Three out of three times I was under the influence. I am still embarrassed and ashamed to admit this.

I went through a mental breakdown. Surprisingly, it was well controlled. I mean it could have been worse than what I actually experienced. I never had closure. I did not feel safe. Being in denial of what happened to me was how I dealt with it. I had no choice. It was my fault; I was the one who allowed myself to be in these situations.

I thought I was with people I could trust. I accepted what happened to me in order to move past what was really destroying me. I never talked about it in detail and not even with my best friend.

Not even God.

Being raped was shameful. I was not in control of my own body, and I did not protect myself. I didn't fight back. You want to know what else I did? I forgave each of them. Why? For my peace and sanity.

There were many things I did that I am not proud of doing at that time in my life. I know it may sound crazy, but I do not regret most of the risks I took or the memories I created that were good and bad. I accept them as lessons learned. I never imagined sharing my story. I decided to expose my most degrading secrets. We usually do not recognize the mistakes we made until they are done.

I cannot say that it was all my fault. I just made sure I acknowledge what I did wrong. Feeling sorry for myself was not going to heal me, and it was not going to change what happened. I could not allow my past to chisel away another lively part of me.

After my mom passed away, my grandmother raised my two younger brothers and me. I was 4 months from turning 16 years old and my brothers were just a few months from turning 11 and 12 years old respectively. I continued to go to school, but I was no longer that A/B student. My attitude changed. Deep inside I knew I wanted love, closure, and an understanding of why. Why me? Why us? Why did my brothers and I have to lose our mother? She was only 32 years old. I did not have anyone to blame. I definitely did not have answers. I was empty and lost.

I not only began to live without my mother, but I also took on a great responsibility of trying to be a mother and a sister to my brothers. I began to help provide for them, help them through school, and be there for them.

I was a protector. I could only protect. I could only teach them as much as I could comprehend. I was not ready to raise pre-teens and teenagers as a teenager myself. I still tried. As all this was happening, I was selfish at times because I wanted to experience life too.

Some people understood I was an inexperienced and irresponsible child.

Regardless, I did my best to balance fulfilling my needs and caring for my brothers. I am thankful for the fact I was able to help care for my brothers. We did not have to separate or leave our home.

Being raised by our grandmother was a blessing. Some days, I could lay my head in her lap and cry. She would comfort me and pray for me. She did not even ask what was wrong. She just showed me unconditional love. She was fierce but so gentle and compassionate.

I was trying to take on a huge responsibility. I was responsible for my brothers. I tried to fill a void in my brothers that I could not fill within myself. I wanted my brothers to know I loved them. We were one. Part of my downfall was I wanted to have fun. That was how I escaped the reality of what was happening around me.

I struggled with being the same good girl vs. the new me. It is so cliché, but I was looking for love and acceptance in all the wrong places. I spent a lot more time hanging out with the bad crowd. Thank God for my praying grandmother. I would frequently visit church with her, and this truly helped me stay grounded.

On bright, sunny and hot summer days, I would be dressed to go out with my friends, but I had on a housecoat so my grandmother could not see how short my shorts were. One day, I snuck out the back door, ran through the alley, and met my friends at the corner. My grandmother could see me from the front door as I jumped in my friend's sister's drop top forest green Sebring. Was it really that serious?

Don't get me wrong. I was not a horrible teenager, but I should have not done a majority of the things I was doing. My grandmother did her best to teach me and support me. She loved me. She knew enough that she was dealing with a complicated, hormonal, and broken teenage girl. She never made me feel that way. She always gave me hope.

In high school, I didn't consider participating in the nursing program, but a friend at the time talked me into taking the class. By the age of 19 years old, I became a licensed practical nurse. I absolutely loved it.

It's funny that I chose to have a career in nursing. My nurturing nature was useful. I found my passion. I was convinced I found my calling. Nothing in my past or present at that time interfered with this opportunity.

Around 2001, I met the love of my life, Keith, during my second year in nursing school. After 3 months of dating, we conceived a child. I was so happy and excited. I did not tell many people. I was definitely not ready to tell my grandmother. When I was ready to tell her I was pregnant, she was in the hospital. She looked me dead in my eyes and said, "I already knew".

Unfortunately, it did not last. I had a miscarriage in my first trimester. I was devastated due to another love loss. Then, two years later, I buried my grandmother on my 21st birthday.

In my mind, I was cursed. Everyone I loved I lost or would lose. This was my mindset. I tortured myself every waking day and every sleepless night. I believed it was my fault that anyone around me died, even if I was not around. I took on the emotional blame of something that was totally out of my control. Could you imagine believing everyone you love you will lose, it's your fault, and you couldn't get over it?

For years, I carried the hurt and pain of my past. The things that happened to me molded me to feel angry, lonely, useless, and desperate. I let people take advantage of me in many ways just to feel important and useful. I accepted treatment that was less than what I was worth just to keep people in my life, so I wouldn't be alone.

I did not know how to let go of my hurt. I did not know what I wanted to gain from attention that I longed for either. I guess I just wanted someone to care. Actually, I really wanted my mother back: The one thing I could never have again.

There were so many days I would hide from everyone, reminisce about my mom, curl up in a ball, and cry until the tears stopped flowing. You never want to forget someone who is so close to you such as a parent or child. I distracted myself so much that I have misplaced memories. Yes, misplaced. I just cannot remember.

I have suppressed many memories. I have had conflicted thoughts. Am I still good enough? Am I worth it? What do I deserve? Is it my fault? How do I right my wrongs? So, I decided to write my wrongs.

Something inside of me keeps me strong when I am ready to break. I had a skill to absorb emotional pain, break it down, and redistribute it in a constructive manner. I adapted because I wanted to be strong for my two younger brothers. Remember, I'm still trying to be a big sister and mother simultaneously. As the older sister, I had to set an example for them and not show my pain. It was my responsibility. I wanted my brothers to be hopeful and to know everything would be okay.

I did what I thought I needed to do for my brothers and myself without hesitation. It was the one thing at that time of my life I felt I did right. I was actually prepared to do it long before I knew it needed to be done.

I sometimes wondered if I was festering a false belief. I could not accept that things would not be okay actually. I knew the consequences of all the choices I made. From the day my mother died on February 11, 1998, I questioned everything I did. I was so insecure. I wondered if I made my mother proud in the heavens. I felt ashamed when I did things that I know she would not approve.

I experimented with the power of choice. I made the choice to take risks, make mistakes, and have fun. By day, I was *the* prudent student. At night and on weekends, I was a wild child. In a sense, I wanted someone to rescue me from myself. I wanted someone to understand me and to simply care for me. I wanted to understand what was happening to me.

My life was complicated. I was so busy hiding from my issues rather than getting help. I honestly did not know where to go and how to ask for what I needed. I did not know what my actual issue was besides losing my mother, grandmother, and first child.

I chose to do things I would do if my mother was alive. I do not regret everything I have done, but my rationalization was not logical. I took risks, but I have some incredible memories and stories to tell! I was full of potential, but I devalued myself with the distraction of my freedom and desperateness for love.

After so many years, I gradually learned how to stop abusing myself with broken relationships, drugs, and alcohol. I stopped using my mother's death as an excuse for my misbehavior. I finally took responsibility to start living and stop avoiding the root issue.

During my battle as a confused teenager with inappropriate behaviors and attitude, I wanted to be better. I wanted to heal. For many years, I battled with who I was in the present and who I envisioned myself to be in the future. I questioned what I wanted. Before I could accept that I was good enough, I took the easy road and allowed myself to be careless.

I chose to be loose. I chose to be irresponsible. There were no expectations. It worked for what I was doing, but I was not comfortable because I really was not like everybody else.

Have you heard the saying "If you spend time with 9 broke people, then you will be the tenth?" or "Birds of a feather flocks together"? These sayings hold so much truth. It was sometimes unbelievable to me that I was not living to my full potential. I felt intimidated to socialize with people I considered to be better than me. That, my friend, was a reason I could not be better than what I was. I disqualified myself.

I did so many negative things that I could not find the good in myself. I felt there was no good within me. What a huge lie! I could be happy and positive for others but not myself.

Our beliefs can make all the difference in our reality. *What we think is not as powerful as what we believe.* Our thoughts are actually led by our beliefs. For example, if I believed that all men are horrible cheating beings, then I will probably attract those types of men. I will anticipate them being the same as the one before. Well of course! What I focus on and believe is what I will manifest. With that same energy, I could expect greater things *and* believe in greater things.

Once I realized this theory, I began to make slight changes in my life. The victory of the healing process was a long haul. Many people know that, just when you are on track, something in life just happens. This can make things more difficult, or it may distract you. The key is to know why you are making a difference within you. Life is not perfect nor easy.

I went to school to become a nurse and eventually things started to change. In 2004, I was pregnant again. My first love and I gave birth to our first son in February 2005. Wow. Three days after my mother's death anniversary, I have a reason to smile again. I had to get out of my feelings of neglect! I definitely had to change my attitude. I am a mother now. Guess what? Three years and three days later, I gave birth to my second son while I was going to school to become a Registered Nurse. I did not mourn my mother as I did before because now I have two reasons to live, love, and laugh like never before. With the love around me now, I still did not feel complete. I quickly realized my children were not born to create my happiness. That was up to me. I was so proud to be a mother. I still am grateful to be the mother of four amazing beings. I made many mistakes in life, but they are my redemption.

As my children start growing, the level of their learning advanced. I started to wonder: How can I expect them to do things I am not willing to do myself? How will they know what success looks like if I do not show them? How can I teach them something I never did like to follow my dreams? Obviously, these were my own personal issues.

Yesterday will come and go, but, when it leaves an impression on you, yesterday may linger much longer than you need it to. It is important to learn from our experiences. My yesterday took me through an emotional rollercoaster. I had to be realistic of the matter. What happened cannot be changed. I had to decide to move on and heal.

Many times, we are approached with life's challenges. We as people may endure similar circumstances and different outcomes. We all have the strength to make the best of our misfortunes if we choose to do so.

We have all heard stories of someone who has endured a horrific or challenging experience. Too often, we give credit to that person being "lucky". We discredit ourselves having what it takes to overcome the challenges we face in our own lives.

I want you to take a moment to reflect on your past. What is holding you back? It may be something that you are intentionally or unintentionally suppressing. Either way, what benefit does it serve you? As you reflect, right now in that moment I am with you. I am giving you permission to let it go! We both know it does not mean you will forget, but at least you can release the chain.

Once yesterday is gone, we now have the opportunity to move forward. Unfortunately, we do not move forward because we spend so much time looking back. Looking at what we could have done differently. Truth is, once a situation happens, we obviously cannot take it back. We should learn from yesterday and make tomorrow better.

Excuse Your Excuses

I have learned not to dwell in the past. You cannot make it far, and you cannot have advancement in life holding on to the past. That is a heavy burden to carry ahead. Why weigh yourself down with something that hinders you from your peace?

Life cannot be predicted. Our circumstances do not define who we are or who we will be. Instead, our reaction to these circumstances fills in the gaps of why we are who we are. That choice is ours.

Yesterday is no longer in your way. It has come and gone. It is one less excuse. So, stop using why you cannot, why you do not or why you have not. Today is now. Tomorrow is near. It is okay to leave yesterday behind.

Lakhila Tellis

The strength you have today comes from your yesterday's pain; your success today comes from yesterday's mistakes.

~ Frank Adofoli

Chapter 2

Choices

The art of choosing; power of choosing.

Choice is such a valuable privilege. As a young, impressionable teenager, I made a lot of wrong choices. I cannot deny it. However, I had to learn to be responsible for my choices. Can you do the same?

The greatest part of my healing was learning to accept responsibility for my own actions. When a person continues to pass the blame and does not acknowledge their role in a situation, it is difficult to grow. We make mistakes at any age. *The magic happens when we learn from those mistakes.* Our mistakes become a part of us, but they do not define who we are.

Character is built from our constant behavior. After observing human behavior in response to situations, we do not realize what psychological damage we do to ourselves. It is frightening how we talk to ourselves and how we treat ourselves.

For example, a person involved in an abusive relationship will blame themselves for the abuser's actions. The abused will believe he or she deserves to be mistreated because they did not perform or act as the abuser has demanded. An abuser will manipulate the victim to feel inadequate and insecure.

Another example is the couple that decides to cheat on each other. They tell themselves it's okay for the other person to cheat because they have a backup plan as well. Now, obviously, this is an unhealthy relationship. Rather than ending the toxic relationship, they stay together and continue to make each other miserable.

Choice. We choose to stay in these situations. We choose to tell ourselves that "I am wrong", "I deserve to be mistreated", and "This is love". Why am I saying this or why the heck am I talking about right now? Well, I was one of these people.

I worked at a nursing facility and a

young lady arrived to work that morning. I could tell she had not slept. She had been crying and fighting during the night into the early morning. She had scratches on her face. Her hair was not styled like her normal upkeep, and her eyes were swollen. I looked in her eyes, and I saw fear and hurt. I saw myself. I pulled her into my office, and we talked. I gave her words of encouragement and let her know she did not have to endure this pain. I did not judge her. I truly could empathize with her. I had drunken fights with my significant other and could barely hold it together. I wished someone would save me. The thing is...I had to save myself. It was up to me to make that choice. That is exactly what I told her. When she was ready, she would make the decision.

I experienced toxic relationships. No one could tell me it was not love. I became dependent on my relationships despite the emotional disruption. I accepted disrespect. I accepted jeopardizing my career. The worst of all was the potential of being the reason my children's lives were chaotic and dysfunctional. I absolutely could not accept that.

I had to change my environment. I made it a priority to be a better person. I did not want to be a perfect person. I wanted to be a more responsible and attentive person. This was not easy. Responsibility is not fun. Although, it is necessary. It seems like it should be a no brainer whether you are a parent or not. This is not the case though.

Having the capacity to make your own choices is so powerful. Yet, we take it for granted. We allow other people to make choices on our behalf, even if we disagree. Why do we allow someone to have this power?

We yearn for this sense of belonging whether it is a conscious or subconscious desire. We do not want to upset or disappoint the other party. We do not want to be embarrassed or fail. When we allow someone else to make decisions, they are the scapegoat when the decisions fail. This is so far from the truth. We are just as responsible for our indirect decisions.

I have always had a passion for learning about psychology and sociology. It is very intriguing to understand human behavior and learn what makes us do the things that we do. Nothing is greater than learning about human nature especially when you learn the nature of your own humanity.

According to Maslow's Hierarchy of Needs, we require basic needs, psychological needs, and self-fulfillment needs that must be met. It is how we have a mental balance. Our needs must be met holistically to have a healthy balanced life. At the base, we must have our basic needs met such as shelter, food, water, and then safety needs such as security.

Next, we enter the need for intimate relationships and being loved. If we do not excel at finding love or feeling accepted, we then struggle with moving upward to the next level. The next level is having self-esteem and feeling accomplished. What many of us fail to learn is that loving yourself is the best intimate relationship to experience.

Self-awareness is a major key in life. Knowing who you are, knowing your limits, and knowing your boundaries can lead to major success or failures. Sometimes we are aware of our personal flaws, but our self-esteem is so low that we destroy our opportunity of success because we believe we may fail or do not deserve the reward.

In the process of healing, I became aware of the stages of life I did not develop so well. I focused on strengthening my weaknesses. The first step of acknowledging my issues was most beneficial. We have the option to either be better or to let issues destroy us. We have the option to hide or fight.

Do not be opposed to facing who you are and who you used to be. Do not just focus your attention to the characteristics that upsets you the most. Highlight even the smallest attributes you love about yourself. Be aware there is more to you than what meets the eye.

Think about this: you can be aware of specific behaviors about yourself, yet you dwell on the negative and you let that overtake you. You let your history overrule what you can become, who you can become. One of my favorite sayings is from Alexander Hamilton: "If you stand for nothing you will fall for anything".

Excuse Your Excuses

That is so true. If we do not have and follow some type of rules, ethics, or morals, how can we abide by any principles or standards? We do not have a stable position in our own lives. We do not recognize our worth and do not know what we deserve! How do we expect to receive respect without having legitimate standards to follow or stand by?

One day, as I was watching television, one of the characters said something that hit me hard: *Parental influence defines us.* This is true, but what if the parent is not there to influence us? How much time needs to be invested to be influenced? I believe there is no time frame.

This really intrigued me because I felt like I did not spend enough time with my mother. In actuality, the sixteen years I did get were effective. I experienced situations and heard stories from my mom and about my mom. I knew enough about her that, if I did have a question, I could consider what she would do.

The first important relationship in life is with our parents. The love, trust, support, and bond we desire to have any relationship starts at birth. The lack of or presence of these desires molds us.

Our environment shapes a part of who we become. Our circumstance influences who we are by the response of our actions to a situation. It is not our circumstances past or present that define our character.

On the flip side, what about those who were not raised by their parent(s)? What influential reasoning defines who they are or have become? *Ding! Ding! Ding!* It is the same process. People develop character from their choices and are influenced by their environment. There are actual characteristics we have in our genes, and we cannot just filter them out.

Two people can be raised in the same environment, with the same issues, opportunities and same memories. Yet, one may have a totally different perception of their reality. That person may see the best of the situation or may be inspired to do better despite the circumstances. The other person may take the situation and just roll with it. They may be angry, resentful, and rebel against any possibility of being better than their circumstances.

Perception and choice make the

difference. I believe that no matter what the circumstance is. You have the ability to turn it into something great or useful. I like to believe this is one of my unique skills. Being optimistic is a difficult ability.

It is a must to recognize you have the grand power and privilege of choice. You may or may not have experienced an unforeseen circumstance that paralyzed you with fear. Your response and the outcome are merely an experience. It is your choice how and when to react to the situation. It is your choice to avoid the situation or face the situation head on.

It was my choice to attract people who needed me. I was attracting people that I could help financially, emotionally and physically. Any way I could help, I was available. This is not always a bad thing, but when you are so busy pleasing others at any cost, you lose yourself.

I was feeding my need to be useful, desired, and loved. I realized I was not going about things the right way. I was draining my spirit and energy more than I was fulfilling it. I was not loving myself.

Over the years, I have worked hard to

reconnect with my true self. I started going back to church, reading personal development books, listening to audios and surrounding myself with people who had common interest and positive vibes. I started making choices for me with my best interest at heart. Initially, I thought I was selfish, but the reality of me saving me was to start thinking about me and giving to myself. I made the choice to accept my errors. You have to choose to do the same. Choose to forgive. Choose to make subtle changes. Whose choice is it for you to have peace?

I made positive choices in my life when I was going through the loss of my mother. I also made not so great choices. I take great pleasure knowing I am here today to help someone like myself to be a voice of inspiration and hope.

I struggled with accepting me being a better person because of a few of the mistakes I made in my past. I refused to allow my past to infect my future. Do not ever think or believe that you are not good enough or undeserving because of past choices. It is a waste of your time.

It is difficult to make choices. Everyone

has the right to do so. With choices comes consequences or rewards. A lot of times the hardest part is weighing out the options we have in front of us. I believe in making choices with good intentions and not only to benefit myself. Remember that your choices may come with sacrifice.

Pick your struggle: doing what is best for you or doing what is best for everyone else? It is up to you to make necessary changes to live a peaceful and fruitful life. Do not confuse doing for yourself as never helping others or only being self-serving. This change is to lead you to take care of you in a self-loving manner. Embrace it.

It is uncomfortable to change. That discomfort is damn sure worth it when it is for the improvement of self. The great power of choice goes hand in hand with being accountable for your actions as well. I noticed there are people who make choices but blame others for their negative results or outcomes. Yet, when positive results or outcomes happen, they take all the credit. How is that even possible?

If this is the case, then we are saying someone else has control of our decisions. Receiving advice and deciding to follow it is a choice that we make. Now if we do not like the outcome, it gives us no right to ignore our responsibility in the matter. If you accept advice, then be ready to accept the result of your action.

We must learn to take ownership in the decisions we make. Assuming responsibility for your life is necessary to take on life's challenges. Accepting our own decisions affects how we survive in relationships. We cannot control people or situations, but we have control in how we handle people and the situations.

There are situations where no choice is the best answer, and that is okay. I need you to focus. Your responsibility is to choose what you think is best. Everything does not deserve a response.

There are choices we have made that we are not proud of. The thought of those decisions haunts us. What is done is done. At some point, we must realize our choices create our future. If you choose to stay in the past, your future will look no different from your present. When you decide to move differently, even slight changes bring about big modifications to your life.

Excuse Your Excuses

When you go through things in life, it is hard to believe it will get better. If you continue to believe that things will not get better, then they will not. I chose to stop abusing myself. I chose to live for me, love me, and be happy! I accept the things in life I cannot change, and I do not allow someone's actions, opinions, or attitudes determine my happiness! Choose to be happy. Try it at least once. It feels so great. Take a lot of moments in your life and free yourself! Be free of anger, free of disappointment…just free! The option is for you to take.

Start eliminating those distractions that are invading your mind and disrupting your progression. It is not too late to create the life that is designed for you. I know you have seen it before: A vision of who you want to be and how you want to live.

Interestingly, through my process of writing this book and indulging in self-development, I have learned much more about myself. With learning, there are levels of understanding. I was digging deep to develop this book. I had to release suppressed memories. I had to be honest with myself. I used my mother's death as an excuse for a lot of choices I made. In reality, I was likely doing what I wanted to do regardless of her physical presence or not.

I struggled with smoking. I started smoking at the age of 12, which my mother knew nothing about. I experimented and enjoyed it. I did not have a bad home life or lack of support at home. Of course, I knew better, but it was what I decided to try and continue to do. Once she passed, I did it more often.

We often like to use our situations for an excuse to justify our mistakes or wrong doings. *Have we stopped to consider that some choices we made are inevitable because of who we are deep inside?* I say this not to judge or be negative. I bring this up to help you realize your inner power: The power you can only control if you accept responsibility and accountability for your choices, no matter how you believe they were influenced.

The power of healing includes understanding and acceptance. Our circumstances are details in our life story that grooms our character. Once the character is developed, the story is created and led by this character. You have every opportunity and right to create a happy character who lives happily ever after. You are the writer, illustrator, and editor of your life story.

You cannot expect change if you do not make the choice to do so. Differences are scary. It is uncomfortable. Differences can also be the best thing you do for yourself, your business, or relationship. Fear of the unknown interferes with many making a great difference.

What changes can you make now? Minor changes can lead to a major impact. Consider taking responsibility for your choices. It may help you make your decisions more wisely. Most importantly, know you have a choice.

Lakhila Tellis

When you make a choice, you change the future.

~ Deepak Chopra

Chapter 3

Love Yourself

Affection based on admiration, benevolence, or commitment.

How dare I have the audacity to think that I did not deserve to write a book? Who would want to hear my story? Why did I believe or think that no one needed to hear my story? I allowed those negative thoughts to distract me.

It took time to gain the confidence I have now. I improved my self-esteem through reading and surrounding myself with better people who encouraged me instead of belittling or judging me. These were huge changes. I had a desire: a burning flame to reignite the passions that are inside of me. I developed a love for myself, so I had to share with others who struggled with loving themselves.

Unfortunately, many people strut around like they are happy, based on their financial wealth, fake happy homes, or their professions. Truth be told, they are likely the unhappiest. Loving yourself will help you have healthier relationships in intimacy, family, work, etc.

I made the choice to stop living in emotional pain and enjoy life in the present and not the past. I was so bitter and sad that I could no longer cry at the saddest situation. I blocked the emotion that allowed me to even cry. I could not even cry for joy.

It took some time to develop my self-esteem and self-awareness. I had to get out of the denial and anger stage in my life. I confused myself into believing I was mighty enough to endure the physical and emotional abuse in my relationships.

I endured the pain for many different reasons. One reason was because I was used to it. Second, I felt like I was needed to help the men in my relationships. I was the one who could change them. I could not help myself.

Once I was truly fed up, I let go. I did not punish myself for loving someone who did not love me in the same respect. It took almost 2.5 years to rebuild and repair myself. You cannot give up on yourself. Forgiveness is for your own healing. I forgave those who hurt me purposely. I forgave whoever hurt me by default. I forgave myself.

We carry baggage of broken relationships, disappointment, lost love (loved ones), and failures. We carry the weight of sadness, loneliness, and blame ourselves for being the source of our problems. We are no good to ourselves or anyone else if we keep carrying the same baggage to every relationship we develop.

I had to find a way to let go of my sadness. I was comfortable being sad. I forced sadness upon myself. I would literally make myself think about all the bad things that happened to me physically and emotionally. Looking back, I admit that was absolutely miserable.

I was blessed to change my surroundings, my friends, and my behaviors. I started spending time with people who appreciated life and happiness.

Ultimately, I wanted the same thing too. I simply wanted peace. I gained genuine happiness.

I remember crying and praying many nights begging for peace and happiness. Yet, I did not know what that was for me. I started reading more books like this. I realize happiness is what I make of it and what I choose for it to be. I do not allow any person to take my peace and happiness from me. It is my responsibility.

I remember being at an event and getting so emotional. The speaker was a remarkable visionary. He spoke such kind words, although this particular time it was regarding a negative incident. The reaction of strangers who had nothing to do with what happened is what made me cry. I cried tears of joy. What brought me to tears was the kind gestures of strangers in response to the incident. I was surrounded by love.

It was so incredibly uplifting to feel genuine love, peace, and gratitude of strangers. I cried more because I was never the girl or woman who was able to share tears of joy or excitement. Usually, sadness and grief could bring me to tears. I knew then I reached a major breakthrough in my life.

If there was any advice I could give anyone, it would definitely be to accept yourself first and love yourself simultaneously. You are just as amazing, incredible and awesome as your idol. You deserve all that your heart and soul dreams to achieve in life.

I perceive dreams as visions created and casted within us before ever knowing what they actually mean. We have a position in this world to serve a higher purpose. We are born with a plan unknown to us, but it develops as we become wiser.

I know you have felt a desire within you to be spectacular and legendary in your own sense. I cannot believe you are not aware of what you want in life. I am sure you have daydreamed about quitting your 9 to 5 and being rich or living fabulous. No one dreams about how hard it will be to achieve greatness. We visualize the end result.

Success scares us most of the time. We

are so afraid of failure that we will not even attempt to achieve or plan our goals. Our minds are cultivated to process fear in the event of the unknown.

As you adapt to loving yourself, prepare for the test of your will. You most certainly will face challenges that are familiar. Your reaction to these moments will be the revealing source of your growth. You should notice these changes as you progress. Be proud of loving yourself. You deserve it. I love when I meet people and they can see my happiness. I worked a job doing phone triage. It was a pleasure to simply answer the phone and people knew I was smiling. They complimented me when I answered the phone by letting me know they were happy to speak with me.

I will never wonder what I would be like if I did not change. There is not one reason for me to question why I love me. It is a process that I work at daily. It is normal to have a bad day but just let it be a moment. Life does not magically become easier or perfect. It does become more enjoyable when you love yourself inside out.

Excuse Your Excuses

Take risks to achieve your dreams. Put in the effort to learn how to be successful in your journey. Step out of your square of normalcy. Love you enough to believe in you. No one will ever believe in you as much as you do. Your high belief will inspire others.

The mistake we make is that we wait on someone else's approval. Well, I am here to tell you that only you can make it official. Get to know yourself and embrace your true quality, skills, and flaws. Our flaws are sometimes not as bad of a quality. They can be corrected or controlled if we choose to do so. Accept who you are and become the ultimate you. It starts with one simple act. Make the decision to love yourself!

Once you master loving yourself, your outlook on life will change. It is inevitable. You accept responsibility for your happiness. How can you look for someone or something to determine your happiness when you do not know how to love yourself?

You have the power to control your happiness. Do not allow anyone to have the sole power to navigate your destiny, peace, and beliefs. It is more than okay to love yourself. Loving yourself is a necessity.

We were born to win and programmed to lose. Only a few people master the art of living and loving life. Stop wasting time wondering if you will be accepted. No one is perfect, so who can we compare perfection to? We should not compare our value to anyone.

I love the following saying by Dr. Seuss: "Those who mind don't matter, and those who matter don't mind". Simple, but deep. My interpretation of this is merely those that are important, supportive and vital to me will understand me and appreciate me as I am. These are the people I want in my loop.

I struggled trying to fit into any particular group or clique. Actually, I still do. I do not like being limited to anything. I have a colorful personality. I love that quality within me. I believe limiting oneself to fit into one particular group strips part of your personality and individuality because you hide what is not accepted or understood by others. I cannot be subject to one box or classification.

Excuse Your Excuses

My passion for becoming a nurse came from my desire to help people. I love people, and I love to help people. I also love having fun, being with family, and enjoying life. I enjoy teaching and leading others to the passion hidden inside themselves. This is how I am fulfilled. What are you passionate about? Is it writing, music, dancing or something else creative? Is it playing a sport, educating or cooking? What fulfills you?

Use your passion to fuel you. Having a healthy hobby will get you through difficult times. You may find peace in doing what you enjoy. Find time for yourself. We wear many hats in life that come with different titles: parent, friend, boss, sister, brother, etc. We find a way to accommodate to fit each role. When we do, sometimes we do not leave room to fit our own personal hat. We often become more consumed in a specific role. We have an imbalance in our personal position in our own lives.

It takes many purposeful decisions to become a better version of yourself. They say you cannot become something you are not. Love yourself, it is okay. I practice positive reinforcement by words to stimulate my mind. I enhance who I truly am. On my journey, I started reading books that helped me gain confidence and share it. I began to find my true self who had been lost for so long. Being genuinely happy and in peace feels marvelous.

I spent many years crying and suffering in horrible relationships with significant others, friends, family, and jobs which wore me down. I decided to be the change I needed in life.

We have conversations daily with people: friends, strangers, family or colleagues. Often, we use the opportunity to converse to satisfy the two Vs: venting and validating. We want someone to hear our side of a story to relieve what is nagging us or to take our side in a situation that is bothering us. How often do we have a conversation with self to clear our conscience? The answer: Not enough.

Why do we trust the opinion of others more than our own perspective? What makes someone else's opinion more valuable than our own? A great part of loving yourself is thinking for yourself and trusting yourself.

Even our body talks to us. Think back to your first crush: that person made you feel a certain way. Maybe you got butterflies in your stomach when they came near you. You knew they were going to that party. So, you chose to endure the heavy thunderstorm and go to the party just to see them. Then, POP! You get a flat tire from a huge pothole! Your gut told you to stay home, but butterflies now have you on the side of the road in the pouring rain. Get in tune with yourself.

I noticed a different outcome when I listened to myself. Most of us are aware of our physical response to situations, but not many pay attention to it. I had to make a conscious decision to follow whatever my gut was leading me to do. I gained confidence in my own judgement doing so. I trusted that I could make appropriate and effective decisions. That extra confidence then strengthened my self-esteem. It was important to not lean on others to lift me up when I was already strong enough to stand alone.

Now do not think you should not

confide in anyone. Make sure the person is a credible, trusted source. What you take in is just as important as who you receive it from. At the same time, realize your thoughts and feelings are just as valid as the opinions of others.

Self-love is rewarding. Everyone deserves to experience the phenomenon of feeling whole. You can choose to be happy. It is a lot of work, but it starts with the decision to not allow anyone or anything to take you out of your element. Loving yourself is filled with many components. It is your responsibility to love yourself. Take accountability for protecting yourself. We cannot hide from the negativity that is in the atmosphere, but we can control what we allow to affect us.

Invest in yourself. Invest real time and money. I am not saying you have to break the bank but sacrifice to make you the better version of you. Invest in saving time to do what you like. Take your mental breaks! Do not worry about what you may need to ignore or what you need to sacrifice to make it happen. Focus on caring for you and strengthening you. Your well-being is so important. It is difficult to complete our daily life tasks if we are distracted by life, tired, and or unhappy!

Free yourself periodically to maintain your sanity. When was the last time you did something for the first time? No matter what, keep pushing. Keep growing. Keep an attitude of gratitude, even when it is your worst day.

True self-love is unmistakable. It is such a free feeling to have a sense of tranquility. It is like when negativity comes your way, a do not disturb sign is there to block it all.

It seriously takes true inner willingness and self-control to maintain this peace. Once discovered, I cannot see how anyone would allow anything to disturb that peace. Self-love starts with accepting your mistakes, flaws, and great qualities all as one. We know there is no one on Earth that is perfect. Do not fear your flaws. Do not allow anyone to make you feel incompetent, unnecessary, or irrelevant.

You are an amazing being. You are loved. You are important. The world needs your personal attributes. You are powerful beyond belief. Tell yourself this every day and believe it! Daily affirmations are needed to build you up the same way negative talk has made its way to tear you down.

Take the time to get to know yourself and understand yourself. Identify your likes and dislikes from A to Z. Identify with your life experiences past and present. Then, visualize your future. Take note of what you want. Literally write your future. Design a plan to reach your goals whether it is to lose weight, go back to school, quit a bad habit, or start your own business. Define and design your desires in life. Believe that you can accomplish these goals. Love yourself enough to give yourself what you want! Plan your future and claim what is yours.

The love you give yourself is warranted. It is not selfish to give to yourself. It is quite the contrary. No one can understand you like you understand your own needs and wants. Until you recognize that, how could anyone else? Love yourself.

Excuse Your Excuses

You need to love yourself and be yourself one hundred percent before you can actually love someone else.

~ Christina Perri

Chapter 4

Unique

A being without a like or equal; distinctively characteristics

What if every book you read had different characters, but the same plot and ending? Would that not be a bit mundane? What would make reading these books interesting if they all say the same thing? It would not be interesting or entertaining, right? So why do you think you need to be like anyone else? Why do you compare *you* to someone that is not you?

I am a unique individual. Does everybody know that? No, they do not. Despite all the hurt and pain, I have endured over the years I stand tall with a great big smile. More importantly, I am extremely motivated to inspire others to choose to smile. I have embraced this skill.

Individuality is what makes all of us unique. Recognizing our differences and similarities are important. Understanding those differences and similarities is what makes us strong. Sometimes we feel so distant that we never feel like we belong.

It has been a while since I contributed to my story. Right now, I was thinking how I was so afraid to live. I let myself become victim to the societal error of trying to fit in. I duped myself by giving a care about what others may think of me. It somewhat matters, but why believe the outcome is negative? I thought about how many people are successful because they did not give up, they did not quit, and they obviously cared. They cared about the benefit of their skill or talent for others versus their own personal gain. It was passion for what they loved to do and desired to become that made a difference.

Once I permitted my true self to lead, I was amazed at how many people responded to me. People that I least expected to understand and recognize my growth gave me fuel to push. The validation of knowing I am headed in the right direction was amazing. I want to share a simple fact: *it is more difficult being someone else and holding back who you were born to be.*

I am continuously working and maintaining myself emotionally, mentally, and spiritually because it is important to me. My unique circumstances created an amazing, fierce woman. I love people who are so unorthodox to the social norm. Some of the most successful beings in the world are unique. They believed in themselves first despite enduring traumatic experiences. They kept fighting despite the negative feedback or being told you cannot or should not. The lovely part is they did not let those moments in life obliterate their dreams. They accepted their experiences and used it to help others.

What makes you different? What stands out with your personality? That is important. What are your thoughts? People have similar circumstances and characteristics but may never speak on it. People need a voice to speak up and let them know it is okay to be different. More importantly, it is okay to be you! The world needs you.

To be like no other should be valued. It is a need for us to represent who we truly are in life. We have so many roles and titles that we sometimes lose our identity. Our personality is embedded within us and revealed in our reactions. We are not perfect. We are all special in our own way. No one should ever make you feel like you should change who you are.

Yes, there are people who may have similar qualities as you do. Do they have your exact thoughts, exact passion, or exact intentions? What about your story? You may not be the first, but you can dominate in whatever you have passion in.

What makes a person relatable? It is their commonality. Why is it important for a person to be relatable? Humility goes a long way. Who you are does not put you on a pedestal. It is what you do that does. What makes you relatable is the acknowledgment of your background and your struggles. The acceptance of challenging adversity to reach your goals is a reward within itself.

Who knew the lessons my grandmother taught me growing up would be the same resources I depend on today? I wonder if the lessons I learned were the lessons she intended for me to receive. Her influence is so much more to me now than ever before. She taught me humility, obedience, and faith. I depend on faith in God like I depend on my eyes to drive! There is no way I can keep moving forward and not appreciate the power of His love, grace, and mercy! Thank you, Granny.

Now this is a part of my uniqueness. I received the benefits of these qualities when I acknowledged them. I also am an organized mess, full of ideas, a procrastinator, working under pressure to produce my best work, a great multitasking business woman, and mother. I embrace it all. I am who I am.

I invested time managing my not so favorable skills so I can use them effectively. I even learned to avoid permitting those skills from interfering with my goals. Working on yourself is not a difficult task. Having the will to improve is the greatest challenge. Do not continue to be stagnant. Why are you letting yourself disengage from your unique purpose?

It is a known fact that collectible items are usually rare, hard to find, and highly desired at a hefty price. However, not all collectibles are worthy. The price people will pay for a rare or unique item substantiates how valuable an item will be. Now apply this fact to your life. Why is it not okay for you to be different? The most famous, successful and popular people are typically those who embrace their gift whether it is a talent, skill or just personality.

Embrace and enhance your uniqueness. Embrace that you are worth more than you can calculate. Understand that you are important. Your thoughts and ideas are valid. You can make a difference in your life and others. Find balance in what makes you great.

Life would be boring if we all were the same. If we all had the same story to tell, who would want to listen? You stand out because of your ability. You stand out because of your strengths. You stand out because of your story!

How many burger restaurants exist?

Lakhila Tellis

There are thousands of burger restaurants across the globe. Some are liked more than others. Some are chain restaurants and others are privately owned. Either way, they are thriving because it has something that sets it apart from the other eateries. It is the same with people. We have something that sets us apart from others.

You are definitely one of a kind. Do not fade away in the background. You are the spark that ignites the fire. You are unique. Do not be ashamed. Do not be afraid. A lot of us may have that "It" factor, but we never hone in to it. Well, take your unique ability or skill to the ultimate level. Go be great!

Excuse Your Excuses

Our uniqueness, our individuality, and our life experience mold us into fascinating beings. I hope we can embrace that. I pray we may all challenge ourselves to delve into the deepest resources of our hearts to cultivate an atmosphere of understanding, acceptance, tolerance, and compassion. We are all in this life together.

~ Linda Thompson

Chapter 5

Be Great

To identify with; remarkable in magnitude, degree or effectiveness

By now you should have an idea of what you want to accomplish. If not, you should know what you must do. You need to discover your purpose or your passion and put all your effort towards it. Let go of the past. It is not easy, but it is worth it!

Throughout this book there are repetitive statements. I purposely shared important key points to emphasize the balance, the change in mentality, and accountability you must acquire to own his or her happiness. I heard repetition is the mother of all skills! It takes repetitive actions and behaviors over time to evolve and to strengthen skills or talent.

Get out of your own way to unleash the greatness you behold. I remember transitioning from nurse to entrepreneur. I admit not being able to recognize my skills. I worked with coaches who basically interviewed me. They asked a series of questions to get to know me, my goals, and why I do what I do. Who knew such simple questions could reveal so much within a person?

Based on my responses to the questions, they could formulate a much more articulate description of my skills. They saw so much in me that I knew was there, but I did not know that others understood it or could see it. I knew my passions but could not figure out how to express them. That alone motivated me to serve my purpose in helping others even more.

You know how you go to the buffet or maybe you have seen someone at the buffet and there is a variety of food piled up on multiple plates? Well this is likely because you have so many options available. Although, you know good and well you will not finish all the food on those plates. You may sample the food and go for more of what you like. You will try foods you do not like or never had before.

Surprisingly, you may keep trying, just a taste, of something you do not like. Initially, you know you do not like it, but your brain says, "It is not that bad, let me try one more time."

Now why is that? Why do we do that? Is it because we paid our money and want our money's worth? Is it because we are just greedy? Is it that we like to experience different things? Well, the answer may be different for everybody. The same person may have a different answer each time.

You must have the same appetite in life. There are so many options in life. Everything you try may not be for you. If you do not go out and learn what works and what doesn't, how can you ultimately achieve anything? You must have that desire and that hunger to go after what you want. Reach for it just like you put that food on the plate. Load up your dreams and goals.

Be realistic about what you want and give every detail of how you want to receive it. I believe in affirmations and manifesting. It will not happen, however, without clear vision and action. You have to participate in making the changes you want to happen.

Embrace the journey to your best self, business, or idea. Upon completion is not what will make you the most satisfied. The personal journey and overcoming the many obstacles along the way is what you appreciate the most.

We make so many excuses of why we cannot do things. Those excuses are usually the exact reasons we should do what we need to do! What is wrong with wanting to do what it takes to give our families and generations a better life? I give you permission to go be great.

Now is the time to be great. Utilize what you have learned. Apply this knowledge to your given skills and experiences. It is not too late to change or go after your dreams. I had a friend who did not become a nurse until she was in her sixties! Even when she retired at 80 years of age, she still worked part time at her leisure. She set a goal late in life, but she achieved it.

Your goals can be accomplished. Do not ever think it is too late. You may have heard of S.M.A.R.T. goals. It is a simple way to remember how to create your goals: **S**pecific, **M**easurable, **A**ttainable, **R**elevant and **T**ime bound. Simple! Create a plan to achieve what you strive for today.

What I came to learn about setting goals is that they did not always get accomplished, or they were not enough to get me where I was going. So, it is not all bad. Having your heart set on specific goals is great but have your mind open to take you higher places. Follow the guidance before you. Do not ignore opportunities. Do not immediately assume that, because things didn't go your way, you have failed. You may be led to a greater opportunity.

I have been through so many challenges like others. I have found that a unique ability I have is to find happiness in every situation. Believe me, it is not easy. Although, it is a natural response. I know the key is mindset.

Shifting your mindset will change your view, your life, and even your environment. You have to be willing to submit to change. Liberate the real and true you. Accept who you are and embrace who you can become. Remember to stay authentic.

One day, I dropped my kids off at school while I was listening to the Rickey Smiley Radio Show as I always do. A recurring guest speaker, Pastor Haynes, was speaking about a gospel song that Rickey had just played. He relates this song to his situation with losing his father. Then, he said something I could relate to. He went on to say, "...not in spite of losing his father, but in consequence was him becoming a great man, a great man of God!"

I recalled a time I actually expected people to feel sorry for me because I lost my mother. I had this strange belief that this is how I should be recognized. I soon accepted that this is not how I wanted to receive recognition. I wanted to be recognized for loving unconditionally and helping anyone I could.

Empower yourself by giving yourself recognition. Acknowledgement of your unique greatness starts with you. Confidence is attractive. It attracts people who will match what you represent. Again, be authentic.

When dealing with people, you encounter various personalities, attitudes, and behaviors. I can endure what most will not. Learning not to take everything personal was important. I also learned that empathy changed how I viewed situations. I do not take it personally. I see people for who they are and not who I expect them to be. It became easy for me to forgive and move on. I chose not to waste time dwelling on the past. I want to control my destiny, my happiness, and my peace of mind.

Once I accepted my true calling, I took full responsibility to fulfill my passion to speak the truth. That was how I would earn recognition. I had to recognize my purpose and passion. You do not just get it. You have to earn it. My mom passing away was not my way to earn recognition.

My mother's death was not my defining moment as a motherless daughter. It may be a part of me, but it was not my character. It did, however, help create my character. Stereotypes are typically created when common ideas are established amongst a group with similarities. Do not allow stereotypical ideals distract your progress.

It is now your time to make a difference in your world. Every excuse of why you should not, why you cannot, and why you do not shall become why you will: Why you will forgive, Why you will move forward, Why you will love yourself, and Why you will be great!

Do you believe you do not deserve peace in your heart and mind? Do you believe you do not deserve love? Do you believe you do not deserve success? By now, you should know you deserve it all. Until you start thinking and seriously believing that you are worth it, you will not have it.

Wake up and keep dreaming. Your ideas are needed. Your love is needed. Your talents are good enough. You are more than enough. You are wanted in this world. Bring your greatness. I challenge you to make an upgrade in your life.

Lakhila Tellis

Every great dream begins with a dreamer. Always remember, you have within you the strength, the patience, and the passion to reach for the stars to change the world.

~ Harriet Tubman

Tips For You

1. Pray.

2. Meditate.

3. Listen to uplifting music that puts you in another zone.

4. Write goals and ideas. All that comes to your mind. This is a simple mental exercise to clear your head.

5. Write in a journal. You are never too old to write your personal thoughts and feelings.

6. Practice Self-Care. Take time for you with or without a companion.

7. Speak positive words out loud to yourself daily!

8. Smile even if you must force it. Think of happy or positive thoughts.

9. Balance the pressure. Do not give up so easily, but do not overwhelm yourself.

10. Breathe.

Get Connected With Author Lakhila Tellis on Social Media

 Facebook.com/LakhilaSpeaks

 Instagram.com/iconic_voice

www.ingramcontent.com/pod-product-compliance
Lightning Source LLC
Chambersburg PA
CBHW021430070526
44577CB00001B/146